I AM **NOT** OLD ENOUGH!

The Twenty-seven Stages of Adjustment to
Living in a Retirement Community

I AM **NOT** OLD ENOUGH!

*The Twenty-seven Stages of Adjustment
to Living in a Retirement Community*

By
Hilde Adler

MODERN MEMOIRS, INC.
34 Main Street #6
Amherst, Massachusetts 01002
413-253-2353
www.modernmemoirs.com

For all my old friends
(who live cheerily in their houses or condos)
many of whom have wanted to know
every last detail about life "over there."

And for all the new friends
I've made in the retirement community,
many of whom have lived through
a few or a lot or perhaps almost all
of these twenty-seven stages.

THE TWENTY-SEVEN STAGES

1. I am not moving anywhere. I love my house. I can handle it. I am not going to live in an apartment.

2. I am not old enough.

3. I don't want to live with all those old people.

4. So maybe I'm as old as some of those people but I look younger.

5. And I certainly act younger.

6. This is a really nice apartment. I hope the person ahead of me on the list doesn't take it.

7. What am I doing with this apartment? This was a terrible mistake. I'm giving it back.

8. I can't believe I did this.

9. I miss everything. I miss the birdfeeder. I miss the sun and the rain and the fog at the front door. I miss walking around my block. I miss the "delicate" feature on my washing machine. I miss my quiet dishwasher. I miss the white pine. I miss the annoying

chipmunk that was so determined to live in the downspout. I miss my friends. I miss the whole neighborhood. I miss the comfort of being where I belong.

10. They have endless social events here. I'm never going to any of them. I'm not social.

11. I will never eat in the dining room.

12. People are really nice. I don't have one thing in common with any of these people.

13. I am never going to take the bus.

14. Somebody wants to have breakfast with me in the dining room. I'll do it just this once. I don't want to be rude.

15. I had a great time.

16. I think last fall was the first time I've ever really enjoyed the fall colors, because I knew I wouldn't have to rake about five million leaves.

17. I'm going to be in a play. I got a great part.

18. What in the world am I doing here?

19. There are no bats in the retirement center.

20. I took the bus.

21. Some of these people have led amazingly interesting lives.

22. I had a great conversation in the dining room last night.

23. I joined the activities committee. We're planning some terrific programs.

24. My right knee hurts. I'm glad there's an elevator.

25. They're predicting six to ten inches of snow. I don't care. We have a heated garage.

26. One of my old neighbors invited me for coffee. I miss my old neighborhood and my people.

27. I think I'm very glad I moved here.

Dear Reader,

TWO THINGS.

IMPORTANT!

PLEASE READ:

First thing: This book is written in two voices, both mine: normal blathering me and *Reality Check*. Normal blathering me is my everyday voice, letting it all hang out, reacting to the moment, declaring this and that with abandon. *Reality Check* is an inner, more sensible, more informed voice which surfaces now and then, most often saying things like, "Give me a break, get real, stop thinking like such a jerk." Sometimes *Reality Check* remains silent. Now and then *Reality Check* just explains how things work in a retirement community or makes a suggestion. *Reality Check is always written in italics.*

Second thing: These particular twenty-seven stages are written from my point of view, which may not be like your point of view at all. I loved my house and hated leaving it. Maybe you didn't feel that way about your house. Or maybe your last home wasn't a house but an apartment or a condo or a trailer or a boat. Maybe you already downsized years ago. Maybe you hated the way your neighborhood changed. Maybe everything was different for you. Maybe whatever. And another thing, I have come to love my retirement community. This did not happen overnight. It crept up on me. And it does not happen to everybody.

Whatever your situation, I hope you can relate to at least some of the feelings expressed in this book. They are universal. Sort of.

Moving to a retirement community is a big deal. It's a major life change. It's finally admitting to yourself that things are not going to be the same anymore! That you've lived a lot of years. This is scary. But it is what it is.

Love,

Hilde

1. I am not moving anywhere. I love my house. I can handle it. I am not going to live in an apartment.

Are you kidding me? I am absolutely not moving to a retirement community. I am not moving anywhere. I'm staying right here in this house.

I love this house. Everybody loves it. This is where everybody always wants to be. I am not leaving here. The children would never forgive me if we sold this house.

It's a great house. It has an attic and a basement and it even has a screened porch. We spend spring, summer and fall on that porch, eat almost every meal out there. There's no way I'm ever going to give up that porch.

And the house is in really good condition. Yes, it's old, but the furnace is brand new and those old-fashioned radiators provide the best kind of even heat, everybody knows that. The roof is brand new, too. We had the entire thing replaced after a hailstorm a few years ago did all kinds of damage to the shingles. Almost everybody in the neighborhood had to have their roof replaced. And they finally fixed that place where the ice dam built up and caused water to leak into the bathroom every winter. It hasn't leaked there in three years.

That big white pine in the front yard was two feet tall when we planted it, after an ice storm knocked over the spruce that was there before. That was some ice storm, people still remember it. There were live power lines down all over the place. We all slept in sleeping bags in front of the fire for three nights, till the power finally came back and the furnace started up again. The whole thing was quite an adventure.

And we have such terrific neighbors. We've been so lucky about those neighbors. They'd help in a heartbeat in the middle of the night if we needed them. They'd be shocked if we left. You don't find a lot of neighbors like that these days, a person would be crazy to give them up.

Besides, it would be just so difficult to live in an apartment. It would make me feel claustrophobic. Think of everything I'd have to get rid of if we moved to an apartment. How could I possibly go through everything in the attic? What would I do with all the stuff we can't take along? The whole idea is too overwhelming; I just do not want to do it. I am not doing it.

And I haven't even mentioned Julius. Yes, of course he's still madly in love with me after fifty-five years of marriage, but he does NOT want to move, he will not move, never, never, never. Never. He's made it clear. If I move, I'll be doing it without him. He will not live in an old age home. (Of course I'd never consider an old age home, I'm not sure these even exist anymore. It's hard to explain the difference between an old age home and a retirement community, especially to Julius, who refuses to listen to anything what-soever about the subject.)

Anyway, I'm perfectly able to do everything I've always done, there is simply no reason to move. I have no problem going down the basement stairs to throw in a load of laundry. So my knees hurt a little on the stairs, who said life was perfect? Of course I can change my own light bulbs. It's so annoying when the kids yell at me to stop every time they see me climb up three steps on a ladder, there is not a thing wrong with my balance. I can absolutely plant the tulip bulbs, and if it makes me a tiny bit sore all over the next day, who cares? I know exactly what to do about the circuit breakers, the toilet valve, the weather stripping, even the bumblebees in the basement (though I've never been able to figure out how those get in there every single spring). I've done it all, I could teach a class in how to own and maintain a house. And for those very few things that are getting a tiny little bit harder, like the snow or the grass or the leaves, all that heavy stuff, I can hire somebody. That's a lot cheaper than moving.

Reality Check: *Well, everything you've said is probably sort of true. But it's not completely true, or the idea of living in a retirement community would not even have appeared on your radar screen. Why are you even talking about this?*

What about that annoying thought that surfaces every once in a while, suggesting that perhaps there's the tiniest possi-bility that you can't keep up this pace forever? That a day may come when maintaining this house and yard will become a bit much? And about the neighbors——wasn't Phil, across the street, ruminating recently about retiring and moving to Florida? He couldn't have been serious, obviously he's much too young. Anyway, time marches on!

I don't want to talk about this anymore. I am not moving! Full stop. Period.

2. *I am not old enough.*

Of course I'm not old enough. How can I be old enough to live in a retirement community? That's for old people, not me. My mother lived in a retirement community. I am not old. I'm not young exactly, but I am absolutely not old. I'm busy every single minute of the day. There are not enough hours in fifty years for me to do everything I still want to do. I am definitely too young to live in a retirement community.

Reality Check: *Would you please step off your cloud! Has your memory started to fail? Do you really not remember how old you were on your last birthday? What do you imagine the average age is in one of these places?*

But be that as it may, if you ever should decide to move, just be sure you do it during the right window of time. If you had moved too soon (a non-issue, obviously) it definitely would not have felt right. You might have wondered, "What am I doing here?" a little too often.

But too late is almost worse. If you wait till you have an emergency, or for some other reason want to move immediately, your apartment choices will likely be very limited if anything's even available. Plus, the longer you wait and the older you get, the bigger a deal everything becomes. Decisions, stairs, adjusting to a new place, making new friends, participating in new activities, learning new stuff, figuring out how everything works in the new community, all become more difficult. And waiting too long definitely makes it harder to take advantage of everything a retirement community has to offer.

I am not interested in making a single new friend, I have enough friends already. I am not interested in participating in a single new activity. I am not the least bit interested in my perfect window of time. I know exactly how old I was on my last birthday. I am not old enough to move into one of these places.

3. I don't want to live with all those old people.

I like to live in the middle of all the different ages, the way it's always been. The way it's supposed to be. I want to hear and see the kids outside. I wish they'd slow down their bikes a little when they see people walking toward them, sometimes I think they're determined to kill me, and I wish they wouldn't trample all over the crocus, but that's all beside the point. I even like to hear the dogs (except for the one that never stops barking, don't they ever let him in?). We always had a dog till our last one died. We had her for fifteen years, I was so sad.

I'm not even the oldest person on the block. Gertrude on the corner is ninety-six and still lives in her house all by herself and she's doing fine. She has five children in town who hover about, and maybe that helps, but still. Everybody's part of the gang on our block. Everybody comes to the block party on Labor Day.

I don't want to live where it's quiet. I don't want to live where everybody's old and not a single person is young. And where everybody has white hair.

Reality Check: *You may not be quite as old as Gertrude,* *but let's get real, you joined the AARP many, many (many) years ago. Your hair hasn't been jet-black for a long time. And you do not have five children living in town who hover. Also, please stop all this romantic exaggeration about the block. It's just a bunch of houses on a street for pity's sake.*

4. *So maybe I'm as old as some of those people but I look younger.*

5. *And I certainly act younger.*

I am not the kind of person who thinks she's better than other people, really I'm not. I am not a snob, not in the slightest. Nobody's every called me a snob. I'm the epitome of not a snob. But this is different. My situation is definitely different. I simply don't look old and I don't act old and I don't dress old. I don't feel old. The people in the retirement community can't possibly feel the way I do.

Reality Check: *Have you looked in the mirror lately? Do it. Try to be objective. Or ask somebody to take a close-up picture of you and then study it. Better still, take a selfie.*

It doesn't exactly shock me that you're saying all this stuff. That's because just about every single person who moves into any retirement community thinks and says exactly the same thing. Everybody is convinced that he or she looks and acts younger than anybody else in the place. Everybody's sure that he or she is doing more interesting things, thinking more interesting thoughts and altogether living a more vibrant life than any other person there.

And stop being so ageist. Ageist is very closely related to snob, which you claim you are not. Stop thinking about the retirement community residents only as "old people." Think about them as "people!" Many residents in a retirement community have led interesting lives, very possibly more interesting than yours, which might come as a shock, and many continue to be totally engaged with the world. They will share all sorts of interests with you and many are people you'd love to know. Wrap your head around this concept.

The whole scenario of how you look and act in comparison to everybody else becomes a lesson in humility, trust me on this.

6. *This is a really nice apartment. I hope the person ahead of me on the list doesn't take it.*

Because I am, after all, open minded, flexible, forward-looking, realistic and not at all set in my ways, I've reluctantly decided, OK, I'm willing to look at just one apartment. Only looking. Of course I'm fussy. It has to be sunny, the right view, large enough, quite perfect really, or I won't be even remotely interested. Don't get me wrong, I have in no way decided to move, not at all. But I've "activated" us on the waiting list.

Reality Check: *Just be aware that not everybody on the waiting list feels like you. Many people would be so happy to get into the community, they'd be ecstatic with any apartment. Some have had some sort of medical or other emergency and they don't want to stay in their house one more day. Others have simply decided that it's time to live in a place with more support. Still others want to move in early because they don't want to move twice. The scenarios are endless. Keep all that in mind while you're being so fussy.*

I have to admit you had an intelligent moment many years

ago when you put your name on that waiting list and gave the place a deposit way before you were ready to move anywhere. That was a good decision on your part. If you hadn't done that, they wouldn't be showing you any apartments so soon after you "activated."

Well, they've been showing me apartments and of course I've been rejecting them. Fortunately there was something wrong with every one of them. It makes me really happy to reject an apartment. I'm always incredibly relieved after I've rejected an apartment. I do not want to move.

Then one day I get another call and trudge over yet again to check out yet another apartment I know I won't like. But, to my horror, I LIKE it!

It definitely does not have the irresistible view of the woods I demanded, the layout is strange, the size is wrong and it's on the second floor, I wanted to live higher up. But there is something about this apartment to which I somehow relate. For one reason or another, in my secret heart, I can imagine myself living in this apartment. To add to my overall misery, it occurs to me that, even though I have so not decided to move to this retirement community, if I don't take this apartment, they may never show me another one I like as much. This is definitely an unexpected dilemma of gigantic proportions!

Katrina, the marketing representative, tells me that one other person, ahead of us on the waiting list, is also looking at this apartment, but if he rejects it, it's ours. Out of the blue I suddenly, desperately, would like to move into this apartment. How long does this person have to decide? A week? That's a long time.

So I wait and worry, and finally I call Katrina. He hasn't called yet but he has to decide by tomorrow. The following day Katrina calls and cheerily tells me that the other person decided he was not ready. If we still want the apartment, it's ours! In sudden shock, I tell her that Julius (who has somehow taken a liking to the woods behind the place and who completely stopped sulking when he met a colleague from work in the hall when I dragged him with me to look at an apartment) and I and our children and sixty-seven of our closest friends and every one of our neighbors would like to look at this apartment again, how long do we have to decide?

When the time is up, I reluctantly whisper, "We'll take it." Julius mumbles that he'll come.

Reality Check: *Congratulations!*

7. What am I doing with this apartment? This was a terrible mistake. I'm giving it back.

In what moment of complete insanity did I decide to take this apartment? How could I do such a thing? Was I crazy? I'm not ready to move to a retirement community. So what if this is an amazingly excellent apartment, I'm not ready, I never decided to do this. Were they pressuring me when they said, "You have a week to decide and then we'll have to offer the apartment to the next people on the list"? They did say that! Was that when some strange voice inside me surfaced and declared, "I don't want the next people on the list to move into MY apartment?" Did I make an emotional, spur-of-the-moment, completely ridiculous decision?

Well, yes, truthfully, there was a moment during which I was actually imagining our furniture in this apartment. In my head I could see exactly where the purple sofa would look really good and where I'd hang the picture of the organ player on the streets of Rio. But I know that would have happened with any apartment.

There'll be other apartments when I'm more ready, I'm

going to give this one back. I never meant to take it. This is all happening too fast. They'll take it back. The waiting list is really long, somebody else will grab that apartment in a minute.

That, of course, is the problem. I don't want anybody else to grab MY apartment. What is it about that apartment that gives it such a special vibe? I can actually imagine myself living in this apartment.

I don't know what to do. Maybe we should keep it? What if they never show us another apartment that we like this much? Strange, but ever since he grudgingly agreed to the deposit on it, there hasn't been a word of complaint from Julius, what's wrong with him?

Reality Check: *This is a big moment. Call the neighbors and have a party!*

8. *I still can't believe I did this.*

We've moved. We're in. I did it. I'm so glad the move is behind me. It wasn't easy. It was a lot of work, but I did it. And I did it quite well, even if I do say so myself. I now know all the tricks about downsizing, what to do with stuff, whom to hire to help. Actually I have become such an expert at downsizing and moving that it has occurred to me to start a service business to help other seniors move. Good idea.

Once we signed the contract, people from the retirement community worked with us to make the apartment look even better. We got to choose new paint, the light fixtures, floors, everything. We got brand new appliances.

I started to measure. I measured all the walls in the new apartment and then I measured them again. I figured out exactly where all the furniture would go and where I was going to put things. I even had the big carpet from our living room cut to make it fit exactly right for the new space, and it looks perfect! They put a new fringe on it. I planned everything, and it all worked. It all looks great, actually.

On moving day, in three hours our whole house was in a truck. It took even less time to move the furniture out of the truck and into our new apartment. It's amazing how good all the stuff from the house looks in the apartment.

The place actually reminds me a little of our house. I was very careful not to clutter. Less is more. When I establish my senior moving service, one of the first things I'll tell my clients is to get rid of stuff, never to clutter.

Who would have thought? Julius seems almost cheerful. The sun streams through the windows in the afternoon.

It's time to invite all the old neighbors to see the place. I think they'll be amazed. Maybe they'll put themselves on the waiting list?

9. I miss everything. I miss the birdfeeder. I miss the sun and the rain and the fog at the front door. I miss walking around my block. I miss the "delicate" feature on my washing machine. I miss my quiet dishwasher. I miss the white pine. I miss the annoying chipmunk that was so determined to live in the downspout. I miss my friends. I miss the whole neighborhood. I miss the comfort of being where I belong.

I miss everything. I miss the house. The sun came in all day long, there were windows on all four sides. I miss watching the birds at the feeder during breakfast. The chickadees and the cardinals were my favorites, the cardinals because I liked their color and the chickadees because I liked their attitude. I even miss watching the chipmunks, even though they drove me crazy when they ate the tulips. I miss picking up the paper at the front door in my nightshirt. In the retirement center you have to go downstairs to the mailboxes to get the paper and this requires getting completely dressed.

I miss my old appliances. I finally had a quiet dishwasher and now I have to listen to a noisy dishwasher all over again.

I don't like my new washing machine either. Whoever heard of a washing machine without a delicate cycle? It says "easy care" but the necks on my T-shirts are definitely stretching. The V-necks are beginning to look obscene.

But what I really miss are the neighbors. My friends. These new people are perfectly pleasant, but they're not my real neighbors, my old good friends.

"Make new friends, but keep the old,
One is silver and the other gold."

We sang that song in Girl Scout camp a thousand years ago but it's still relevant. I'm going to miss my golden friends for the rest of my life. I miss walking around the block with them after supper on summer nights, looking in the windows of all the houses and checking everyone out. Now I live on a hall where all the doors are always closed. I have no clue what's behind those doors. Probably I never will?

And the neighbors miss me, they've said so. Everybody wants to know what it's like "over there." Some have come by to see the new digs. They promised to visit often, but it won't be the same. A few did start talking about putting their names on the waiting list. The place should give me a commission!

10. They have endless social events here. I'm never going to any of them. I'm not social.

I am so totally not interested in any of the social stuff happening in this retirement community. It's not that I'm a recluse or anything. I like people, actually. But I have absolutely no interest in being social in this place. None. I'm never going to get know these people, I could care less. It's just too much trouble to get to know all these new people who know absolutely nothing about me or the cool things I've done, or anything else about my history for that matter. They don't know and they don't care. I'm not even going to try, it takes too much energy, this is not middle school, I'm simply going to live my life, I don't need or want a single new friend. I have enough friends already. Anyway, as I've mentioned, these people are all old.

Truth be told, I love a good conversation with friends at the kitchen table or in the coffee shop. But I'm abominably, embarrassingly bad at "making conversation." I have never been able to meet people through activities that are organized primarily so that people can meet each other, like coffee hours or mixers. Some people thrive in those, but I don't. They terrify me, to be honest.

I am immensely attracted to the idea of remaining locked in my apartment for at least the next seven years without ever leaving it at all.

Reality Check: *Will you please just stop making pronouncements about everything you're never going to do. You'll get involved because you're not going to be able to resist all the interesting activities that will pull you in to participate. You know you hate to miss a good time. You don't have to go to social hours. Sorry to disappoint you, but if you don't show up at those, nobody will mind and nobody will care and absolutely nobody will miss you. Chances are nobody will even notice because you have not yet appeared on anybody's radar screen. Stop, already, with these illusions of importance.*

Some people sweep fairly easily into the social life in a retirement community, others are a bit intimidated and some are terrified. It's hard to generalize about social life. The truth is that there are going to be people in the new place who really do care to get to know you, who are interested in you and in your life BRC (Before Retirement Community), who are willing to show you the ropes and eager to do things with you.

So relax!

11. I will never eat in the dining room.

Reality Check: *This is closely related to #10. And how that works depends a little on your outlook on life, but more on how the eating scenario in your particular place is organized.*

First about the food. In some retirement communities, the food is totally delicious. In others it's not. Life is unfair that way. Some places serve three meals a day, some serve only dinner. In some, you're expected to eat all meals in a dining room; others provide a "take-out" option where you can pick up the food and eat it in your apartment. For a small fee, they may even deliver it to your apartment. The take-out option allows a way out if you are philosophically not crazy about the concept of eating in a restaurant every night for the rest of your life. Many places have a food allowance, which means that a certain monthly fee is charged for food whether you eat it or not. In addition to all this, almost all independent living units have kitchens. Do you still want to cook? Or never again, not on your life. That's the food part.

Then there's the social part (again). In some places a hostess simply seats you with somebody when you come to the dining room. This is sometimes a good way to meet new people and occasionally it's a disaster. In others, residents make their own dinner dates, some people eat with the same crowd every night and others like to mix it up. Some residents always prefer to eat by themselves with a good book. It takes time to figure all of it out.

I am beyond attracted to the take-out option. I intend to eat with Julius and the *News Hour* and occasionally have a conversation with Julius, if he should happen to be in a talkative mood. I am never eating in the dining room.

12. People are really nice. I don't have one thing in common with any of these people.

I love theater and I'm pretty good on the computer for somebody my age. I hate to cook, have always hated it, baking is even worse. I love folk songs, Joan Baez, Pete Seeger, all that. I love to be outside. I recycle. I like to wear extremely comfortable clothes and sandals or sneakers, and wear real shoes only when there is no escape. I like to sing "The Star Spangled Banner" and I tend to be opinionated about people who run for public office.

Penelope, across the hall, doesn't even do email, which drives me crazy, I'm going to have to teach her some computer skills. She grew up on some farm in North Dakota. She's a weaver. I have to admit, she makes absolutely gorgeous Navajo-style rugs. And she bakes all the time, she says it relaxes her. She makes lemon bars to die for (and she shares). She has her hair "done" every single Friday morning and she always looks put-together. She wears real shoes all the time. She and I have absolutely not one thing in common. But I like her. She's been super-supportive and welcoming. And she has a great sense of humor.

I think Sanford, who lives in the apartment next to mine, is Penelope's boyfriend, but I'm not sure. I'm watching them carefully. I've already noticed that "hooking up" (as they say) is a fairly frequent occurrence in a retirement community. Sanford is a famous nuclear physicist of some sort and seems obsessed with whooping cranes and Mahler symphonies. He's really nice. Elizabeth and Eric, next door to him, are also nice. They are crazed about playing bridge, they play it constantly and seem to win a lot because I keep seeing their victorious scores posted here and there. My game is Scrabble, and I'm still pretty good at Clue. Max and Darlene, at the very end of the hall, have eight grandchildren and fifteen great-grandchildren and they're always either talking about them or having them in their apartment for sleepovers. I have one grandson. This is not an even playing field. I get along just fine with all these people. I wouldn't dare bring up politics with any of them.

Reality Check: *These are your new neighbors and the floor is your new neighborhood. Neighborhoods are diverse, everybody knows that, and we're supposed to like it that way. Peace and good will in a neighborhood are extremely important, I think you learned this or something like it in Sunday school.*

13. *I am never going to take the bus.*

Our retirement community has a (green) bus. It picks people up right in front of the door and goes to grocery stores, out to eat in restaurants, and it even goes to the symphony or theater or to a lecture, and sometimes to a funeral. Occasionally it goes on whole-day trips, to interesting places actually. I think the bus riders generally get off the bus about six inches away from their destination. People sign up for the bus and wait for it in the lobby, they're always early. They all seem to be friends with the driver. Walkers and wheelchairs and any other devices you can imagine seem somehow to fit on this bus.

I want nothing to do with this bus. We have a car and I can drive myself any place I want to go. I'm a very good driver, I hardly ever get a ticket, except now and then I speed a tiny bit, which is because I learned to drive in New York City. Sometimes it's hard to park really close to the theater or wherever I'm going, and I have a sort of long walk. I don't mind that because it's good for me to breathe the fresh air, plus it keeps me in shape. I just mind slightly when it's raining or freezing cold.

I am never going to take the bus.

Reality Check: *Are you ever going to stop saying "I am never"? It's annoying.*

14. Somebody wants to have breakfast with me in the dining room. I'll do it just this once. I don't want to be rude.

While I was riding my five miles on the stationary bike in the fitness center (I started with half a mile and am working my way up to twenty but Heather, one of the fitness instructors, warned me not to overdo), Alice from the fourth floor came in to use the Nu-Step. We managed to talk a little bit, even though we were both quite busy breathing. She suggested the two of us meet in the dining room for breakfast next Tuesday so we could have a better conversation. It would have been really rude to decline so I agreed.

I ordered a double omelet and added every vegetable offered on the list. It was delicious. We had a great conversation. One thing Alice and I have in common is that neither of us has lived here very long. She moved in six months before we did so knows the turf a lot better and she's savvy about almost everything, which I am definitely not. She told me that she had many of the same feelings and misgivings when she first moved in, but she's already really glad she made the decision to move here. We agreed it was an adjustment. We shared all sorts of insights about life here and she gave me some great ideas. She told me she joined a book group and that the discussions are really interesting, I should come and try it.

We talked about some things we might like to do together, like go to the Botanical Garden or the ice cream store. And we decided we're going to meet for breakfast again next week.

15. *I had a great time.*

I did. Maybe I should try dinner some time? Maybe I could pry Julius away from the *News Hour* for just one night and include him? Maybe we could meet somebody brand new?

Reality Check: *You're making a small touch of progress!*

16. *I think this fall was the first time I've ever really enjoyed the fall colors, because I knew I wouldn't have to rake about five million leaves.*

Remember how totally, incredibly gorgeous the colors were this past fall? The maples all looked like paintings, they were spectacular. The autumn colors around here have not been this beautiful in fifty years.

Last autumn, the leaf blower got heavier for some reason and it wore me out. In previous years it was always so much fun to use, even though it was noisy. Anyway, when all the leaves were finally down last year, I hired a company to clean up the yard. They mowed the grass and blew the leaves out of everything, including the flower beds, even though I told them clearly that I wanted to keep the leaves there as mulch. It was so annoying that they never understood that. They came at exactly the wrong time, just before a windstorm, which wasn't exactly their fault, but everything they piled at the curb blew right back onto the grass. And the next day it started to snow. It was exasperating.

I'm almost ashamed to admit it, but this past fall I actually gloated when I drove around town and saw all those lawns covered with leaves. I smiled benignly (hidden from view in my car, of course) at all the exhausted-looking rakers. I toasted the fact that I will never again have to think about leaves or mulch, or even the Creeping Charlie, which is taking over the lawn. Never in my life.

While I was at it, I toasted no longer having to worry about the basement flooding during a bad rainstorm; never again having to deal with a chipmunk in the dryer motor. Squirrels hissing at me from the inside of the garage are a thing of the past. When the toilet overflows I will call "maintenance" and somebody will come to fix it, same if the furnace or air conditioner suddenly stops or if the dispose-all in the sink stops disposing for some reason. Hailstorms making holes in the roof will no longer be my problem. Outside paint can flake and the wood around the front door can rot as far as I'm concerned. I will never again freeze almost to death while using my hairdryer to open the garage door, which has frozen to the cement. "Somebody" will make sure the hot water gets turned back on immediately if it should ever go off. Stress about loose bricks on the steps to the front door and a subsequent lawsuit has evaporated. Water softener salt has become a non-issue, as has the whole-house humidifier. And should I decide to go off on a trip, which I hope to do now and then, the shades can stay up, the lamps will not need timers; I will simply lock the door and leave, and "they" will do whatever it is they do about the mail and the paper. I have been liberated. Cheers!

The fall colors were totally magnificent this year.

17. *I'm going to be in a play. I got a great part.*

I know. I said that I would never participate in any activities in this retirement community. I said it and I meant it. But when I came across this notice in the *Bulletin* (I read bulletins when they are put in front of me, I was a school teacher for quite a while) that someone was looking for residents interested in being in a play, I couldn't help it, I just could not resist. I haven't been in a play since I was little. I simply had to check this out.

A woman who did a lot of theater in her previous life ran the organizational meeting and was going to direct the play. I signed up. Yes, I was willing to come to practices. Yes, I was willing to take any part. I didn't know one other person there, but they all seemed enthusiastic and friendly and, at least on the surface, not at all bothered by the fact that this new person (me) was signing on to this play.

It turned out that the "play" was a series of old radio shows and we, the actors, were divided into various skits. We sat around a table with the scripts, so we could read our parts and didn't have to memorize lines. Memorizing, I discovered, is not always the strongest suit for people living in retirement communities.

I was Blanche Bickerson, from the old radio show *The Bickersons*, starring Don Ameche and Frances Langford. Blanche does nothing but bicker with her husband, John, usually in the middle of the night. It didn't take long for my partner, Roger, who played John, and me to relax, submerge into our characters and bicker with conviction. When I told him that his snoring was driving me totally crazy, I meant it. The play was a hit and I had a fabulous time. I met some kindred spirits, and the best part was that I felt like I was part of the gang. Roger still calls me "Blanche."

Participants in the many activities in our place tend on the whole to be friendly and welcoming. There is one exception to this: the Bridge players. I do not pretend to understand Bridge players. Otherwise pleasant, friendly, jovial people become unsmiling, almost fierce, while they are playing this game. Their entire personalities seem to change when they are sitting at the card table. They pretend you don't exist. They will not say hello when you pass by. They glower if you so much as attempt a feeble wave or a thin smile in their direction. After the Bridge game is over, they quickly turn back into their normal selves and might even wave enthusiastically. It is a fascinating phenomenon. Mahjong players are more relaxed. They will wave even in the middle of a game.

Reality Check: *I hope you realize this conversation is really not about plays, or games, it's about participating. Participating is the secret to feeling that you belong, that you're really a member of the community.*

18. What in the world am I doing here?

This is a really nice hotel and I've had a wonderful time here. But I want to go home now!

19. There are no bats in the retirement center.

In our house we periodically had bats in the attic. I know not everybody in every house has bats, but we did. Bats were always flying around the neighborhood on summer evenings and occasionally they found a way into our attic. We hired a batman, who came in a batmobile, to abate them. But they always came back. I've heard that bats are somehow good for the environment and that they are a protected species, but I hated them, they scared me.

I have not encountered a single bat, or any other creature for that matter, in the retirement community. But if I did, I'm certain that I would simply scream loudly and then call maintenance and they would come and take care of the problem immediately. Comforting!

But this is about more than bats. The bats are just symbolic. It's about all the things that happen in a house that I no longer have to worry about in the retirement community. Like the furnace that stops working for some reason right in the middle of a blizzard; the tall tree in the back yard that sways menacingly every time the wind gusts get over thirty miles an hour, and occasionally loses a huge branch that has to be cut up and hauled away; the spot in the corner of the kitchen ceiling that's always wet and I haven't been able to figure out where the water's coming from, what if it's mold? It's about frozen pipes and a dead phone line and all the other stuff that eternally needs fixing or at the very least needs constant worrying about or thinking about when you own a house. It's about owning property and trying to take good care of it. It's about the ongoing challenge of keeping things up to date and in decent condition.

In the retirement community, somebody else takes care of just about all these things. Maintenance and upkeep issues are no longer my problem, and this is a great relief. Maybe once upon a time I considered house issues challenging and almost fun. But now? Are you kidding?

Reality Check: *I think you're beginning to see a glimmer of light!*

20. *I took the bus.*

Well, we had tickets to the symphony and it was going to be a particularly excellent concert with a huge choir, which I love, and they were predicting a particularly horrible snowstorm. So at the very last minute before they removed the sign-up sheet I signed up for the bus. We waited in the lobby and got on the bus with all the other people.

The bus was warm and cozy. It felt like an ordinary bus. No worries about sliding around at every slippery stoplight. No long walk on icy patches. No freezing. It was fabulous.

Why did it take me so long to discover this bus? This bus has been here, why have I not been using it? Sometimes I think I'm a slow learner. I totally love this bus. Next month, I'm going to sign up early to be sure there's a space for us. Why would anyone want to drive in the winter if they can take the bus?

Reality Check: *You are a slow learner. But keep it up! There may be hope for you!*

21. *Some of these people have led amazingly interesting lives.*

I've been meeting a lot of people since moving to this retirement community but let's face it, we're not exactly meeting each other during the prime of our lives. I don't mean to be disrespectful, but even I can recognize that all of us, even including me, who live in these places are likely to be ever-so-slightly over the top of the hill. Let's get real. There's a chance that we don't exactly look or act the way we did when we were twenty or thirty or even forty-five.

So it's been eye-opening to talk with some of these new people and find out what they really did once upon a time. At this point they don't necessarily resemble my imaginary version of the dean of a business school at the university, or a sex therapist, or a sheriff, or the singing star in any number of local theater productions. I didn't realize at first that I was living on the same floor with a medieval historian, a transplant surgeon, a nurse who helped deliver over three hundred babies, an expert at rewiring old houses or the man who raised the #1 prize-winning cow (I forgot what kind) in the whole county. Somebody on my floor invented a new kind of apple, go figure! Of course there are also ordinary people who just sort of lived their lives, like me. Seeing the apartments of other residents is one great way of under-standing their life stories, but the apartments are so hard to get into. I'll have to do something about that.

Reality Check: *When you were little, your mother taught you something along the lines of "don't judge a book by its cover," so she obviously had this figured out a long time ago. This might be a good time to remember everything your mother told you. Most of her advice will probably work in the retirement community. And keep finding out stuff about the neighbors. If you're lucky they might even get interested in you!*

22. *I had a great conversation in the dining room last night.*

I've been eating in the dining room now and then, even though I swore I'd never do this. I don't know how this happened. Why don't I ever stick to my resolutions?

My neighbor, Penelope, lured Julius and me into having dinner with her in the dining room. It turned out to be quite OK. The server took our order and I didn't have to do anything but sit there. We talked about all the things people talk about: the British royal family, climate change, a movie we've all seen and liked, the Galapagos, restaurants in town, the Green Bay Packers, where we lived BRC, the children, books. And about life here in the retirement community, including the quality of the food. I ended up with a lot of good information. We stayed away from politics, gun laws and immigration. It was all good. I can't believe I'm saying this.

I still don't want to eat in a restaurant every single night for the rest of my life and I remain addicted to the *News Hour*. But I guess dinner with friends in the dining room is OK once in a while. Sitting there and having a server take your order is not all bad. And it really is a good way to meet other residents. Some people do it all the time and somehow seem to survive.

23. I joined the Activities Committee. We're planning some terrific programs.

At our place we have committees for everything. I joined the Activities Committee. I was a gym teacher in a previous life and I think this is somehow related to why I love dreaming up and organizing events and cajoling people to participate. My children would say I love telling people what to do, I should have become an army drill sergeant, as was suggested years ago in an interest test. But that's not true. Maybe it's a tiny little bit true. But the Activities Committee is a good fit for me. A person who was a dietician, a great cook or is just extremely interested in food might want to join the food (or "dining") committee. Someone who was a doctor or nurse might like to get involved in the health care of the place. Some people recoil at the thought of being on any sort of committee. They've "been there, done that!"

On our committee we plan events and carry them out with the help of our staff person. For example, we had a resident art show. Another time, we invited members of our writing group to read some of their original work. We tried a version of "speed meeting" to introduce residents to others they didn't know. We bring in speakers on subjects we think will interest people. We organized a comedy hour (and it actually worked). We had people submit photos of themselves as children, and had everybody try to identify everybody else. Our activities are designed to involve as many people as possible and to try to build community. That's the whole idea.

Reality Check: *It's great that you joined a committee. As you noted, this is not for everybody, but you seem to like that sort of thing. You're lucky they had a place for you. It certainly is a way to become part of the scene. If you ever feel like you've had enough committee, stop. Remember it's your life and you're (yes!) old. You can do what you want.*

24. My right knee hurts. I'm glad there's an elevator.

My right knee has been hurting for a while now. Actually it's been hurting for about twenty years, but it hasn't been hurting enough to demand an enormous amount of my attention until recently. I fell on it years ago when I slipped on some black ice while I was racing to the car because I was late to take somebody to the airport, and it hasn't been the same since. I'm still furious at the person who needed the ride to the airport because it's his fault that I slipped on the ice and fell down and ended up with this problem! Unfortunately he is no longer with us.

It's not awful, I'm not limping and I don't need a walker or a cane or anything, but it just hurts sometimes, especially when I go up and down stairs. Mind you, I can still walk up and down stairs. I cling to the handrail a little but I can absolutely do it. I can even do it when there is no handrail, like outside in a courthouse or another place like that, where I might have to go some time to explain that I have not been speeding, I was simply driving with the traffic. I just have to go up the steps extremely slowly.

I confessed this knee situation to my doctor and he, though usually annoyingly avid in the promotion of exercise, suggested I walk up and down as few stairs as possible and take an elevator whenever I can. He thought it wasn't helping my knee to put weight on it. So, since I am not particularly interested in replacing the entire thing, I always use the elevator now. There are other perks about the elevator. It beats slogging the groceries up the stairs. It's great for moving furniture, like when I wanted to exchange the gray chair that didn't work in the new apartment with the flowered futon I left in my son's storage locker.

In addition, the elevator is a wonderful place to meet people. Since one is virtually imprisoned with others during a ride on an elevator, and since especially whoever is the button pusher has to ask what floors the others live on, one might as well find out who they are, when they moved in, where they came from and as much other information as possible. If there's somebody on the elevator whom I don't know, I always ask his/her name during the ride. Sometimes I even remember their name the next time we meet on the elevator, and if I'm really in good shape that day, maybe I even remember their floor. Then they feel very flattered and think I'm smarter than I actually am, and immediately want to have lunch.

The elevator is also an excellent venue for short discussions. The weather is always a good topic, particularly for those who have just come in from the outside and are in a soaking wet coat with dripping hair. For people who've just been to a program together, a ride in the elevator is just enough time to evaluate. It's certainly enough to determine if the program was good or pretty good or horrible. Now and then I have even asked my elevator mate(s) to come to our place and discuss things further over a cup of coffee or a glass of wine. As I mentioned, I've made some friends in the elevator.

I am very happy to finally live in a place with an elevator.

25. *They're predicting six to ten inches of snow. I don't care. We have a heated garage.*

During the last few years in our house, we hired a snow service so I didn't have to worry about snow removal anymore. Sort of. I still had to do the little stuff around the edges that they never did. And it didn't really bother me much that they sometimes got to our house very late, sometimes not till the middle of the night, or that we were usually the last people on the block to get our driveway cleared. They always got there eventually.

I liked them, they even answered their cell phones from the truck most of the time. I always knew they'd come. But whenever it snowed, I wondered anyway. Will they come? When will they come? Will they remember the part they have to shovel or are they so busy today that they'll just plow and run? Will they remember to sand the walk to the house? We have company coming, we don't want anybody to break a leg or anything. And I don't want to break mine either, spreading the Melt-Away. And will they remember to shovel around the fire hydrant? But despite these misgivings, a snowstorm didn't bother me nearly as much with the snow service as it had when we had to do all the shoveling and snow blowing ourselves.

But if I thought I didn't care that much about a snowstorm then, I really don't care about it since I've lived in the retirement community. Now I look out of the window during a snowstorm and feel totally secure that every inch of the driveway and road has been or will soon be cleared to bare ground and if I have to walk outside for any reason, like if I'm taking care of somebody's dog, or just because I like the snow, I know those walks have been shoveled and salted. The chances of my remaining in one piece on a snowy morning are infinitely higher since I've been living in this retirement community. (No guarantee of course!) In addition, I do not have to race to buy groceries if a blizzard is predicted, secure in the knowledge that in the retirement center I am very unlikely to starve.

And then there's the heated garage. If I had to name only one reason why I'm glad to be in the retirement community, it would without any doubt be the heated garage. I drive into the garage with my car covered with snow and ice, dripping slush, and an hour later or the next morning the car is sitting serenely in its assigned stall, everything has melted, all this miserable stuff has disappeared. Well, it hasn't totally disappeared. It's left messy streaks on the garage floor. And I sometimes wonder if my spot looks particularly horrible and messy. Anyway, every spring they come and clean the garage and all the yellow lines between car stalls miraculously reappear.

When we lived in our house, which had a detached,

eternally icy garage, which I admit is unusually old-fash-ioned and certainly not everybody's situation, the snow and ice stayed on my car until spring. And groceries! Now I wheel them to my apartment in a cart. No more stepping gingerly over this and that ice patch, trying to balance the bags of groceries and sometimes losing the toilet paper down the little incline.

We also have visitor parking in our garage. Everybody who visits us in the winter loves the heated garage. When, every December 31, our (old neighborhood) friends decide that our apartment is the perfect place to celebrate, I'm quite aware that it isn't because of my scintillating personality or Julius' great wisdom. I have no illusions. It's because they know that, not matter what the New Year's Eve weather, at the end of the evening they will remain toasty when they step into their warm car in the heated garage and head on home.

26. One of my old neighbors invited me for coffee. I miss my old neighborhood and my people.

Of course I keep up with the old neighbors. They're my friends and I love them. I miss them. And they love me and miss me too, at least they've said that. So when one or another of them invites me for coffee or tea or supper, or just to talk, I can't wait to go and am beyond excited to be back in the old neighborhood.

Sometimes I stand on the sidewalk in front of my old house, which now belongs to somebody with four small children and doesn't even look like our house anymore with all those toys lying around in the front yard and the big wooden jungle gym in the back, and just gaze at it for a while and remember that I was very happy in it.

That's never going to change. But the thing that has changed over time, maybe six months or a year, or maybe even two or three years later, is that, though I'm as excited and happy as ever to be back in the neighborhood, I'm OK with going home at the end of the visit. Over time, "home" has moved from where I was then to where I am now. This change was so subtle that I didn't even realize it was happening. But there was a moment when I knew it had happened.

My golden friends, and that house, and the tall pine in the front yard—I will love those forever!

27. *I think I'm very glad I moved here!*

Reality Check: *Are you really?*

Yes, I really am!

MANY, MANY THANKS

for suggestions, advice, opinions,
enthusiasm (or not)
and conversations related to this book
to
Julius, David, and Jeane (as always)
and

FROM THE OUTSIDE

Cokie Albrecht
Sally Bilder
Alex and Bill Dove
Bobbie Malone
Mary Trewartha
Cousin Jean
Kitty, Ali, and Vinsula at Modern Memoirs, Inc.
and

FROM THE INSIDE

Joy Knox
Mary Metz
Ginny Shannon
Fred and Judy Whitemarsh
the Oakwood Writing Group
Ann Albert from SAIL

(and all my other invaluable readers!)

ILLUSTRATIONS

Front cover & interior: Dennis Cox/Shutterstock.com